The Afternoon of the Faun

The Afternoon of the Faun

by

Stéphane Mallarmé

Illustrated and in the original French text
with an English translation
by

J. R. PHILLIPS

ILLUMINA PRESS
Pasadena, California

Copyright © 2017 by J. R. Phillips

All rights reserved. No part of this book may be used or reproducedin any manner whatsoever without written permission, except in the case of brief quotations embodied in critical articles or reviews.

Book design by the author. Illustrations by Eduard Manet and Henri Matisse in Public Domain..

Front cover image by Pál Szinyei Merse
Back cover image by William-Adolphe Bouguereau 1873

Portrait of Stéphane Mallarmé by Édouard Manet
from the collection of Musée d'Orsay
Self portrait of author by author

ISBN-13: 978-0998616063
ISBN-10: 0998616060

Printed by Illumina Press
in the United States of America

Illumina Press Inc.
P.O BOX 60444,
Pasadena, CA 91116
626-460-7090

CONTENTS

Illustration by Georges Barbier	opposite page 3
"L'Après-midi d'un Faune	3
Illustration by Édouard Manet	11 & 17
Illustration by Arthur Fischer	13
Illustration by Mihály Zichy	16
Translation by J. R. Phillips	17
Illustration by Henri Matisse	25
Illustration by Margaret Cameron	26
About the Authors	27

Introduction

A popular translator of Gabriel García Márquez, Gregory Rabassa, in an essay titled *No Two Snowflakes Are Alike: Translation as Metaphor* draws attention to some of the most difficult tasks in attempting to translate a recognized literary work to a language uniquely foreign to the native language of the original author. Distinctions such as 1) cultural differences, 2) language structure and stylistics, 3) demographics, and 4) historical perspectives provide an enormous impact on the mind of the reader. Someone writing in the late 19th Century, like Mallarme, would be largely influenced by what is commonly indicative of the early stages of industrialization—the enormous displacement of rural society, the rapid growth and turmoil accompanying the rise of urbanization, the resultant overcrowded cities, environmental pollution, and human alienation. All these conditions are everywhere reflected in the Mallarme's Paris of the 1880s. The future comforts and conveniences these early stages of modernization give rise to must have seemed unfathomable or simply a topic for science fiction. So to incorporate a modern flavor to such writings, as was the tendency of a Pound and a Horace Gregory when exploring the ancient writings of Catullus and or a Li Po, though often entertaining, I find lacking the original intent and historical perspective of the native author's efforts.

As Rexroth once commented: "How much does Proust mean to a Chinese collective farmer and vice versa? Imagine Dante translated by Dorothy Parker or Shakespeare by Tristan Tzara."

In regards to the Faune poem: I believe Mallarme was deliberate in his choice of the pastoral form popularized by Virgil in his *Bucolica* for his subject of the woodland satyr, and, though its meter is far less formal than his Latin counterpart, the dream-like imagery and the musical intonations of the language still manage to capture the essence of classical antiquity and can be seen as Mallarme's attempt to escape the mundane world of modern urbanized France.

So it has been my intent to mirror as closely as possible the near English equivalent of each word, each phrase used by Mallarme as well as sustaining the rhyming metrics so often overlooked by much of the early translators.

One of the earliest translators, Roger Fry, in his 1937 publication of *Collected Poems* did no more than give us a literal transliteration of the Faune poem almost devoid of the all the erotic underpinnings. C.F. McIntyre in his 1959 edition of *Selected Poems* fared not much better. Recent translators like Peter Manson and Paul Herron are much more respectful of the author's metrical intentions and seem much more aligned with the poem's sensuality and erotic suggestions.

Still, it has always seemed a worthy task to focus more closely on this one poem that has, more than any of the efforts of his French predecessors and contemporaries, to epitomize the ultimate culmination of French Symbolist poetry. For it is my contention that *L'Après-midi d'un Faune* is to Stéphane Mallarmé what *The Waste Land* was to T.S. Eliot.

J. R. P H I L L I P S

MALLARMÉ

L'APRÈS-MIDI D'UN FAUNE

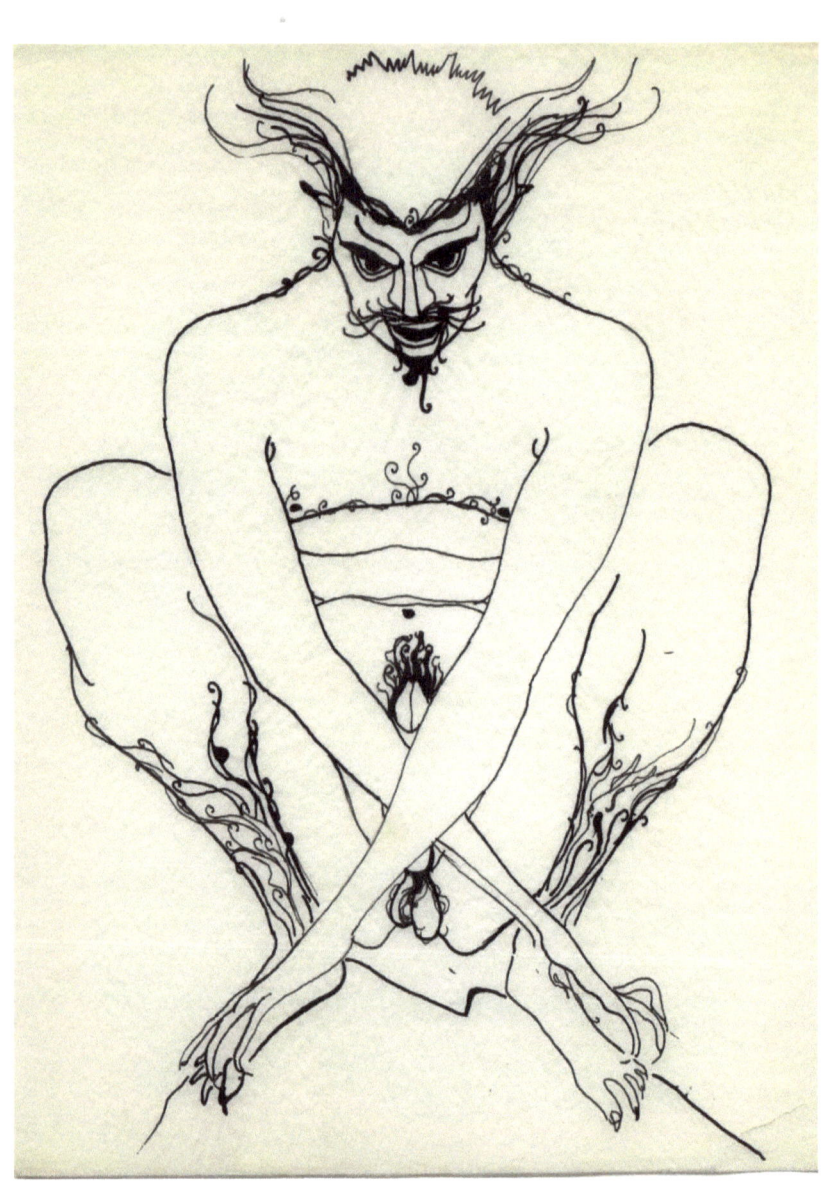

L'APRÈS-MIDI D'UN FAUNE

Églogve

LE FAUNE

Ces nymphes, je les veux perpétuer.

                        Si clair,
Leur incarnat léger qu'il voltige dans l'air
Assoupi de sommeils touffus.

                              Aimai-je un rêve ?

Mon doute, amas de nuit ancienne, s'achève
En maint rameau subtil, qui, demeuré les vrais
Bois mêmes, prouve, hélas ! que bien seul je m'offrais
Pour triomphe la faute idéale de roses.

Réfléchissons..

                      ou si les femmes dont tu gloses
Figurent un souhait de tes sens fabuleux !
Faune, l'illusion s'échappe des yeux bleus

Et froids, comme une source en pleurs, de la plus chaste :
Mais, l'autre tout soupirs, dis-tu qu'elle contraste
Comme brise du jour chaude dans ta toison ?
Que non ! par l'immobile et lasse pâmoison
Suffoquant de chaleurs le matin frais s'il lutte,
Ne murmure point d'eau que ne verse ma flûte
Au bosquet arrosé d'accords ; et le seul vent
Hors des deux tuyaux prompt à s'exhaler avant
Qu'il disperse le son dans une pluie aride,
C'est, à l'horizon pas remué d'une ride,
Le visible et serein souffle artificiel
De l'inspiration, qui regagne le ciel.

O bords siciliens d'un calme marécage
Qu'à l'envi des soleils ma vanité saccage,
Tacite sous les fleurs d'étincelles, CONTEZ
» Que je coupais ici les creux roseaux domptés
» Par le talent ; quand, sur l'or glauque de lointaines
» Verdures dédiant leur vigne à des fontaines,
» Ondoie une blancheur animale au repos :
» Et qu'au prélude lent où naissent les pipeaux,
» Ce vol de cygnes, non ! de naïades se sauve
» Ou plonge..

      Inerte, tout brûle dans l'heure fauve

Sans marquer par quel art ensemble détala
Trop d'hymen souhaité de qui cherche le la :
Alors m'éveillerais-je à la ferveur première,
Droit et seul, sous un flot antique de lumière,
Lys ! et l'un de vous tous pour l'ingénuité.

Autre que ce doux rien par leur lèvre ébruité,
Le baiser, qui tout bas des perfides assure,
Mon sein, vierge de preuve, atteste une morsure
Mystérieuse, due à quelque auguste dent ;

Mais, bast ! arcane tel élut pour confident
Le jonc vaste et jumeau dont sous l'azur on joue :
Qui, détournant à soi le trouble de la joue,
Rêve, dans un solo long que nous amusions
La beauté d'alentour par des confusions
Fausses entre elle-même et notre chant crédule ;
Et de faire aussi haut que l'amour se module
Évanouir du songe ordinaire de dos
Ou de flanc pur suivis avec mes regards clos,
Une sonore, vaine et monotone ligne.

Tâche donc, instrument des fuites, ô maligne
Syrinx, de refleurir aux lacs où tu m'attends !

Moi, de ma rumeur fier, je vais parler longtemps
Des déesses ; et, par d'idolâtres peintures,
A leur ombre enlever encore des ceintures :
Ainsi, quand des raisins j'ai sucé la clarté,
Pour bannir un regret par ma feinte écarté,
Rieur, j'élève au ciel d'été la grappe vide
Et, soufflant dans ses peaux lumineuses, avide
D'ivresse, jusqu'au soir je regarde au travers.

O nymphes, regonflons des SOUVENIRS divers.
» Mon œil, trouant les joncs, dardait chaque encolure
» Immortelle, qui noie en l'onde sa brûlure
» Avec un cri de rage au ciel de la forêt ;
» Et le splendide bain de cheveux disparaît
» Dans les clartés et les frissons, ô pierreries !
» J'accours ; quand, à mes pieds, s'entrejoignent
       (meurtries
» De la langueur goûtée à ce mal d'être deux)
» Des dormeuses parmi leurs seuls bras hasardeux ;
» Je les ravis, sans les désenlacer, et vole
» A ce massif, haï par l'ombrage frivole,
» De roses tarissant tout parfum au soleil,
» Où notre ébat au jour consumé soit pareil.
Je t'adore, courroux des vierges, ô délice
Farouche du sacré fardeau nu qui se glisse,

Pour fuir ma lèvre en feu buvant, comme un éclair
Tressaille ! la frayeur secrète de la chair :
Des pieds de l'inhumaine au cœur de la timide
Que délaisse à la fois une innocence, humide
De larmes folles ou de moins tristes vapeurs.
» Mon crime, c'est d'avoir, gai de vaincre ces peurs
» Traîtresses, divisé la touffe échevelée
» De baisers que les dieux gardaient si bien mêlée ;
» Car, à peine j'allais cacher un rire ardent
» Sous les replis heureux d'une seule (gardant
» Par un doigt simple, afin que sa candeur de plume
» Se teignît à l'émoi de sa sœur qui s'allume,
» La petite, naïve et ne rougissant pas :)
» Que de mes bras, défaits par de vagues trépas,
» Cette proie, à jamais ingrate, se délivre
» Sans pitié du sanglot dont j'étais encore ivre.

Tant pis ! vers le bonheur d'autres m'entraîneront
Par leur tresse nouée aux cornes de mon front :
Tu sais, ma passion, que, pourpre et déjà mûre,
Chaque grenade éclate et d'abeilles murmure ;
Et notre sang, épris de qui le va saisir,
Coule pour tout l'essaim éternel du désir.
A l'heure où ce bois d'or et de cendres se teinte.
Une fête s'exalte en la feuillée éteinte :

Etna ! c'est parmi toi visité de Vénus
Sur ta lave posant ses talons ingénus,
Quand tonne un somme triste ou s'épuise la flamme.
Je tiens la reine !

    O sûr châtiment...

        Non, mais l'âme
De paroles vacante et ce corps alourdi
Tard succombent au fier silence de midi :
Sans plus il faut dormir en l'oubli du blasphème,

Sur le sable altéré gisant et comme j'aime
Ouvrir ma bouche à l'astre efficace des vins !

Couple, adieu ; je vais voir l'ombre que tu devins.

MANET

Satyr and Nymph by Arthur Fischer

L'Apres-midi d'un Faune

The Afternoon of the Faun

Translated by
J. R. PHILLIPS

Eclogue

The Faun

These nymphs, I would perpetuate again.
                                        So bright
Their crimson flesh that lingers there, light
In air drowsy with tufted slumbers.
                                  Did I love a dream?
My doubt, glimmers of ancient nights, ends extreme
In many a subtle branch, that keeps true
The woods themselves, proving, alas, that I too
Offered myself, alone, the triumph of the ideal sin of roses.

Let me reflect....
                or if those women you describe
Mirror your fabulous senses' desire, try
Faun, illusion dissipates those blue eyes
Cold, like a fount of tears, of the one most chaste:
But the other, she, all sighs, contrasts your taste
Like a breeze of day warm on your fleece?
No! Through the swoon, heavy and motionless
Stifling with heat the cool morning's struggles
No water, but that which my flute pours, murmurs
To the grove sprinkled with melodies: and the sole breeze

Out of the twin pipes, quick to breathe

Before it scatters a sound in an arid rain

Unstirred by any wrinkle of the horizon,

The visible breath, artificial and serene,

Of inspiration returning to heights unseen.

O Sicilian shores of a marshy calm

My vanity plunders vying with the sun,

Silent beneath scintillating flowers, RELATE

'That I was cutting hollow reeds here tamed

By talent: when, on the green gold of distant

Verdure offering its vine to the fountains,

An animal whiteness undulates to rest:

And as a slow prelude in which the pipes exist

This flight of swans, no, of Naiads cower

Or plunge…'

      Inert, all things burn in the tawny hour

Unknown by what art there fled away together

Too much of hymen desired by one who seeks there

The *perfect note*: then I'll wake to the primal fever

Erect, alone, beneath the ancient flood, light's power,

Lilies! And the one among you all for ingenuousness.

Other than this sweet nothingness shown by lips, the kiss

That softly gives assurance of treachery,

My breast, virgin of proof, reveals the mystery

Of the bite from some illustrious tooth planted;

Let it pass! A certain secret chose as confidant,

The great twin reed we play under the azure ceiling,

That turning towards itself the cheek's quivering,

Dreams, in a long solo, so we might amuse

The beauties round about by false notes that confuse

Between itself and our credulous singing;

And create as far as love can, modulating,

The vanishing, from the common dream of pure flank

Or back followed by my shuttered glances,

Of a sonorous, empty and monotonous line.

Try then, instrument of flights, O malign

Syrinx by the lake where you await me, to flower again!

I, proud of my murmur, intend to speak at length

Of goddesses: and with idolatrous paintings

Remove again from shadow their waists' bindings:

So that when I've sucked the grapes' brightness

To banish a regret done away with by my pretence,

Laughing, I raise the emptied stem to the summer's sky

And breathing into those luminous skins, then I,

Desiring drunkenness, gaze through them till evening.

O nymphs, let's rise again with many memories.
'My eye, piercing the reeds, speared each immortal
Neck that drowns its burning in the water
With a cry of rage towards the forest sky;
And the splendid bath of hair slipped by
In brightness and shuddering, O jewels!
I rush there: when, at my feet, entwine (bruised
By the languor tasted in their being-two's evil)
Girls sleeping in each other's arms' sole peril:
I seize them without untangling them and run
To this bank of roses wasting in the sun
All perfume, hated by the frivolous shade
Where our frolic should be like a vanished day.'
I adore you, wrath of virgins, O shy
Delight of the nude sacred burden that glides
Away to flee my fiery lip, drinking
The secret terrors of the flesh like quivering
Lightning: from the feet of the heartless one
To the heart of the timid, in a moment abandoned
By innocence wet with wild tears or less sad vapours.
'Happy at conquering these treacherous fears

My crime's to have parted the dishevelled tangle
Of kisses that the gods kept so well mingled:
For I'd scarcely begun to hide an ardent laugh
In one girl's happy depths (holding back
With only a finger, so that her feathery candour
Might be tinted by the passion of her burning sister,
The little one, naïve and not even blushing)
Than from my arms, undone by vague dying,
This prey, forever ungrateful, frees itself and is gone,
Not pitying the sob with which I was still drunk.'

No matter! Others will lead me towards happiness
By the horns on my brow knotted with many a tress:
You know, my passion, how ripe and purple already
Every pomegranate bursts, murmuring with the bees:
And our blood, enamoured of what will seize it,
Flows for all the eternal swarm of desire yet.
At the hour when this wood with gold and ashes heaves
A feast's excited among the extinguished leaves:
Etna! It's on your slopes, visited by Venus
Setting in your lava her heels so artless,
When a sad slumber thunders where the flame burns low.

I hold the queen!

                    O certain punishment…

                                    No, but the soul

Void of words, and this heavy body,

Succumb to noon's proud silence slowly:

With no more ado, forgetting blasphemy, I

Must sleep, lying on the thirsty sand, and as I

Love, open my mouth to wine's true constellation!

Farewell to you, both: I go to see the shadow you have become.

Matisse

ABOUT THE AUTHORS

STÉPHANE MALLARMÉ

Mallarmé was born in Paris in 1847. Like Baudelaire before him he has ranked not only among the top French Symbolists of his era, but has also been credited as a having a major influence on the advent of Literary Modernism of the early Twentieth Century.

The poem, "L'après-midi d'un faune" written between the years 1865 to 1867 has often been considered his literary masterpiece. So much so, it has been rendered musically by the Impressionist composer Claude Debussy and followed up with a controversial interpretation by the Russian *enfant terrible* choreographer, Vaslav Nijinsky in 1912.

J. R. PHILLIPS

A Los Angeles resident since the age of four, Mr. Phillips began serious study in the art of translation while attending graduate classes under the tutelage of Berkeley professor Dan Bellm at the Los Angeles campus of Antioch University.

He has been published in numerous literary journals, authored four books of poetry including translations of the French of Raymond Radiguet and Charles Baudelaire. He has created over thirty video poems, one of which was selected for the 2014 Visible Verse Festival in Vancouver Canada in October 18, 2014.

ILLUMINA PRESS

…On the composition by Claude Debussy the composer writes:

The music of this prelude is a very free illustration of Mallarmé's beautiful poem. By no means does it claim to be a synthesis of it. Rather there is a succession of scenes through which pass the desires and dreams of the faun in the heat of the afternoon. Then, tired of pursuing the timorous flight of nymphs and naiads, he succumbs to intoxicating sleep, in which he can finally realize his dreams of possession in universal Nature.

And the poet's response in a letter addressed to the composer:

I have just come out of the concert, deeply moved. The marvel! Your illustration of the Afternoon of a Faun, which presents a dissonance with my text only by going much further, really, into nostalgia and into light, with finesse, with sensuality, with richness. I press your hand admiringly, Debussy.
                                    Yours, Mallarmé

www.ingramcontent.com/pod-product-compliance
Lightning Source LLC
Chambersburg PA
CBHW041823220426
43666CB00004BA/60